Daniel And The French Robot

Daniel's Toys

Today, just like every day, the French robot said hello in French as soon as he saw that Daniel was awake:

Today the French robot wanted to teach Daniel how to say some toys in French.

So he wrapped some of Daniel's toys so Daniel could guess what the French words meant!

The first thing the French robot brought out was **un ballon.**

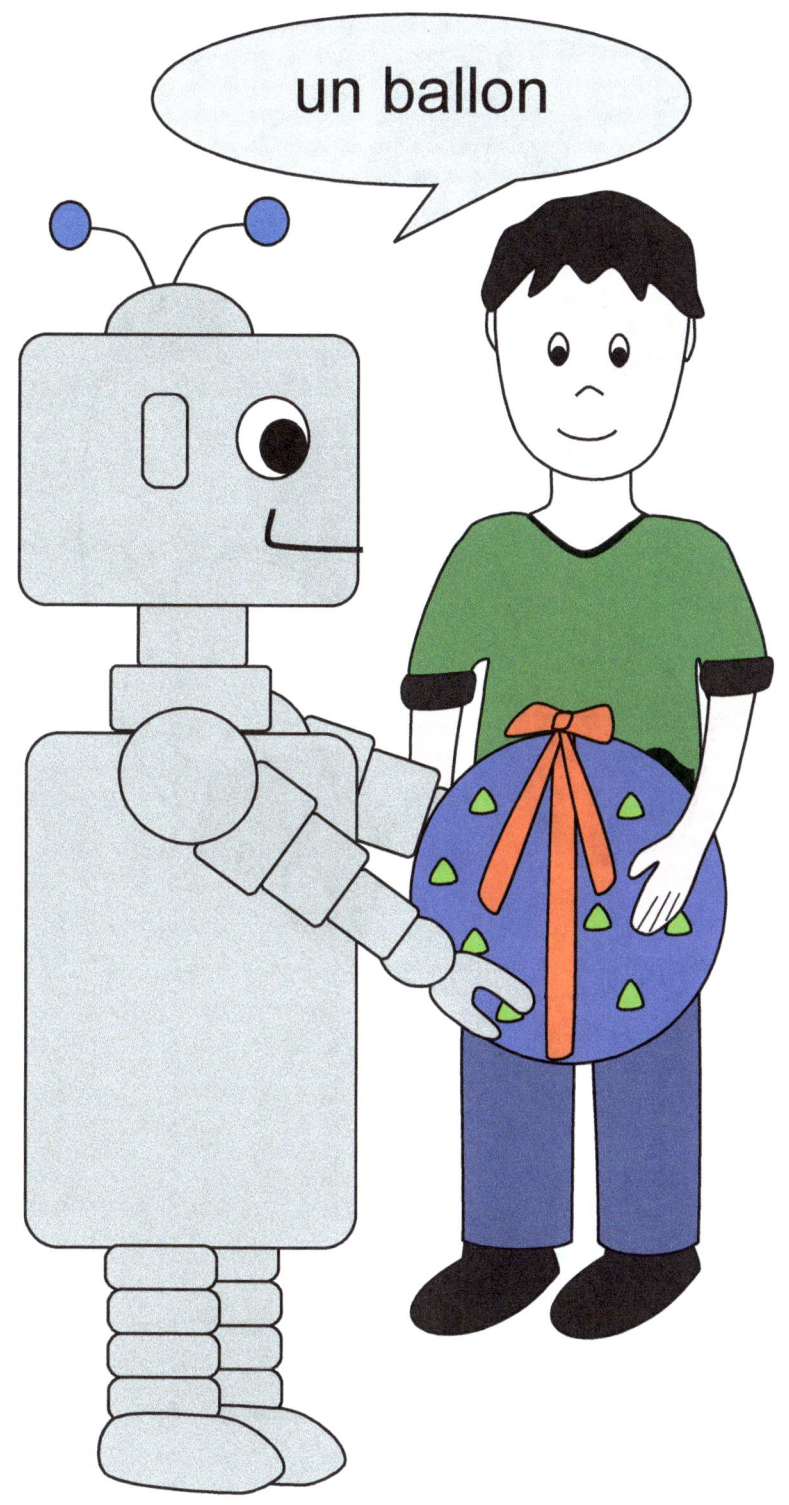

Daniel carefully felt the shape. He then quickly unwrapped it to find.....

un ballon

Un ballon was a ball!

Yes! He was right!

The next thing the French robot brought out was **un nounours**.

It was soft.   It had two legs and two arms.

Daniel carefully unwrapped the parcel to find….

un nounours

Un nounours was a teddy!

Yes! he was right again!

The next thing the French robot brought out was **une poupée**.

It was soft. It had two legs and two arms. He only had one teddy that was like that! Not knowing what it was he unwrapped it to find….

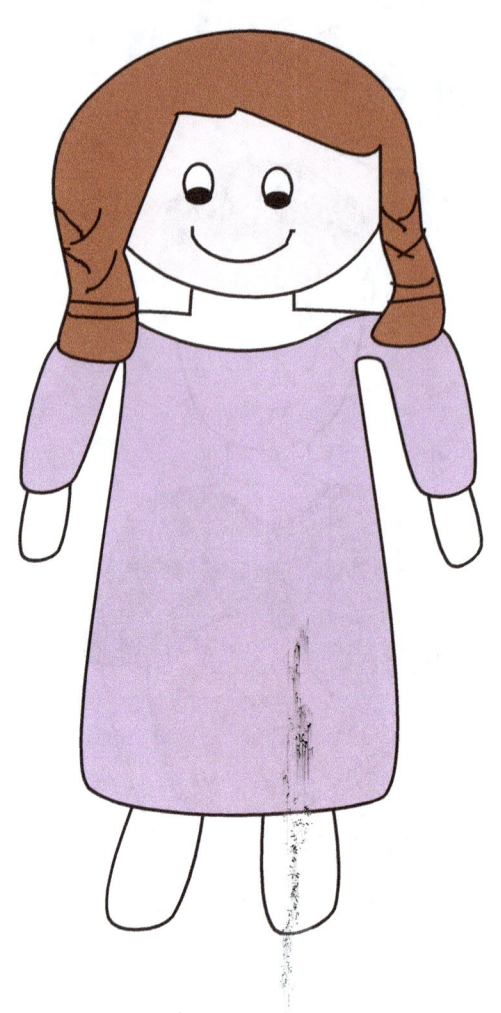

une poupée

Une poupée was a doll! A DOLL !!!

"Hey! That's not mine!" thought Daniel. "My cousin must have left that when she was playing here yesterday!"

The next thing the French robot brought out was **un bateau**.

Daniel felt carefully the shape.

Daniel thought he could recognise this toy.

He unwrapped it to find....

Un bateau was a boat!

Yes! he was right!

For the last object the robot led Daniel into the back garden:

This time Daniel didn't need to feel it's shape. He knew exactly what it was! He ripped off the paper quickly to find…

Un vélo was a bike!

Yes! he was right again!

It had been a fun day. Can you remember all the French words for the toys? Let's say them together!

un ballon

un nounours

une poupée

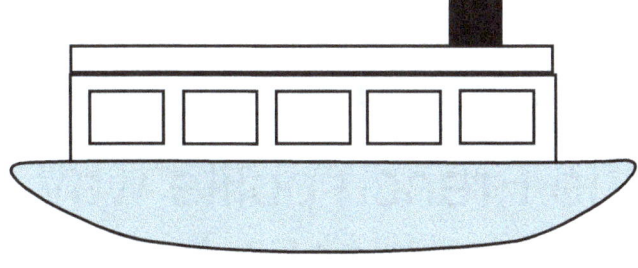
un bateau

un vélo

Now Daniel knew how to say his toys in French he could ask the robot for his toys:

Un ballon, s'il vous plaît.

The French robot was very pleased that Daniel had remembered the French word for a ball and that **s'il vous plaît** was the French polite way of saying please, so he went and got a ball.

They both then played together in the garden until Daniel's cousin called round for the doll she'd left at Daniel's house yesterday. Daniel was now able to tell her that **une poupée** was the French way of saying a doll.

Daniel And The French Robot

Daniel Helps Père Noël

It was a cold December morning when the French robot got an urgent message from **Père Noël**:

Père Noël needed help! The French robot went quickly to get Daniel. Father Christmas must be *very* busy. So they needed to help **Père Noël**!

It didn't take long to get to where **Père Noël** lived as the robot could fly there. When they arrived the robot saw a beautiful Christmas tree so he told Daniel to look at the tree:

Daniel said in French that it was pretty. The truth is though he found *every* Christmas tree pretty! **Père Noël** looked happy to see them. He greeted them with a friendly "**Bonjour**".

Père Noël wanted to check he remembered all the French words for some toys. Let's say them with Père Noël:

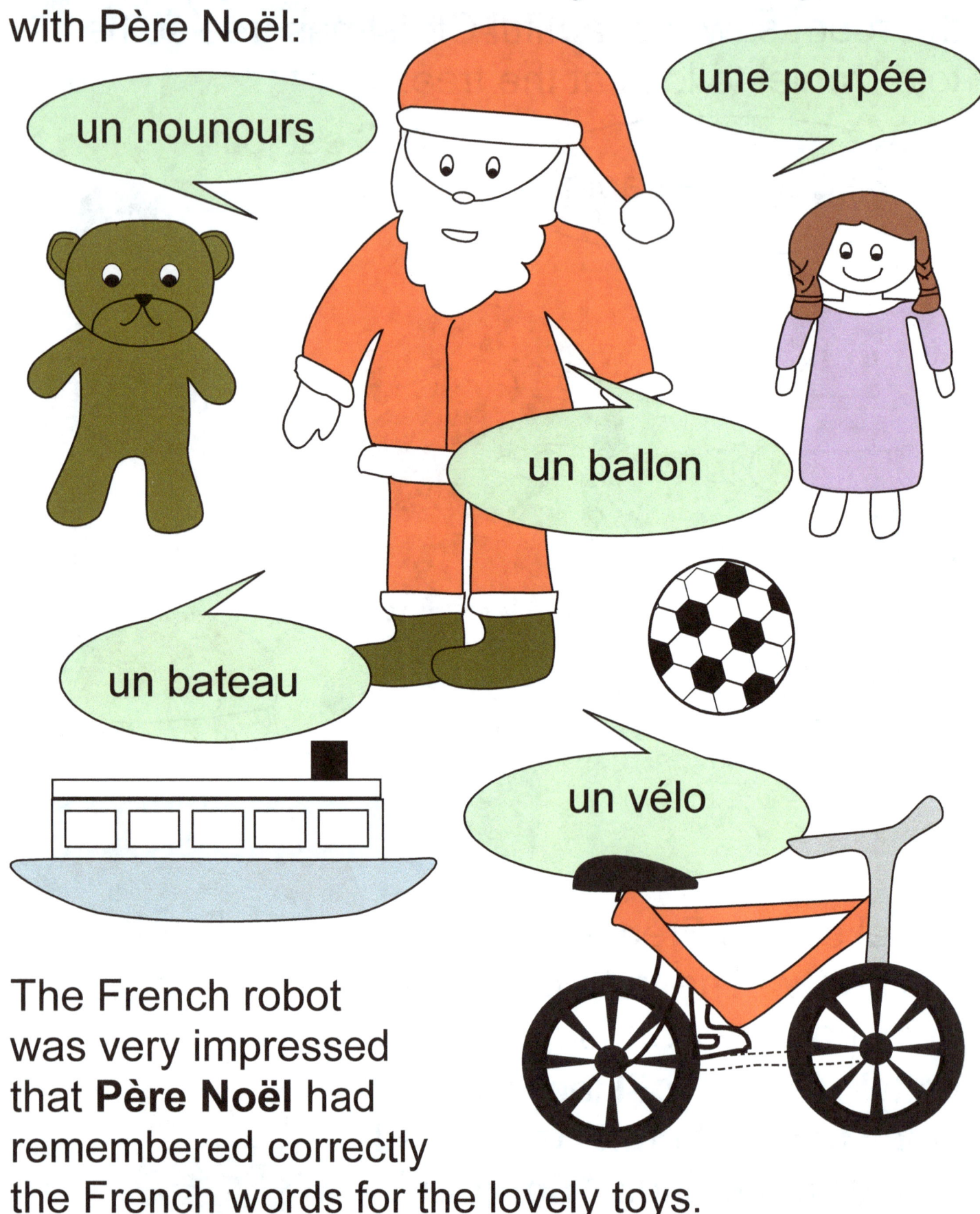

The French robot was very impressed that **Père Noël** had remembered correctly the French words for the lovely toys.

The first thing they were asked to do was to count how many scarves there were:

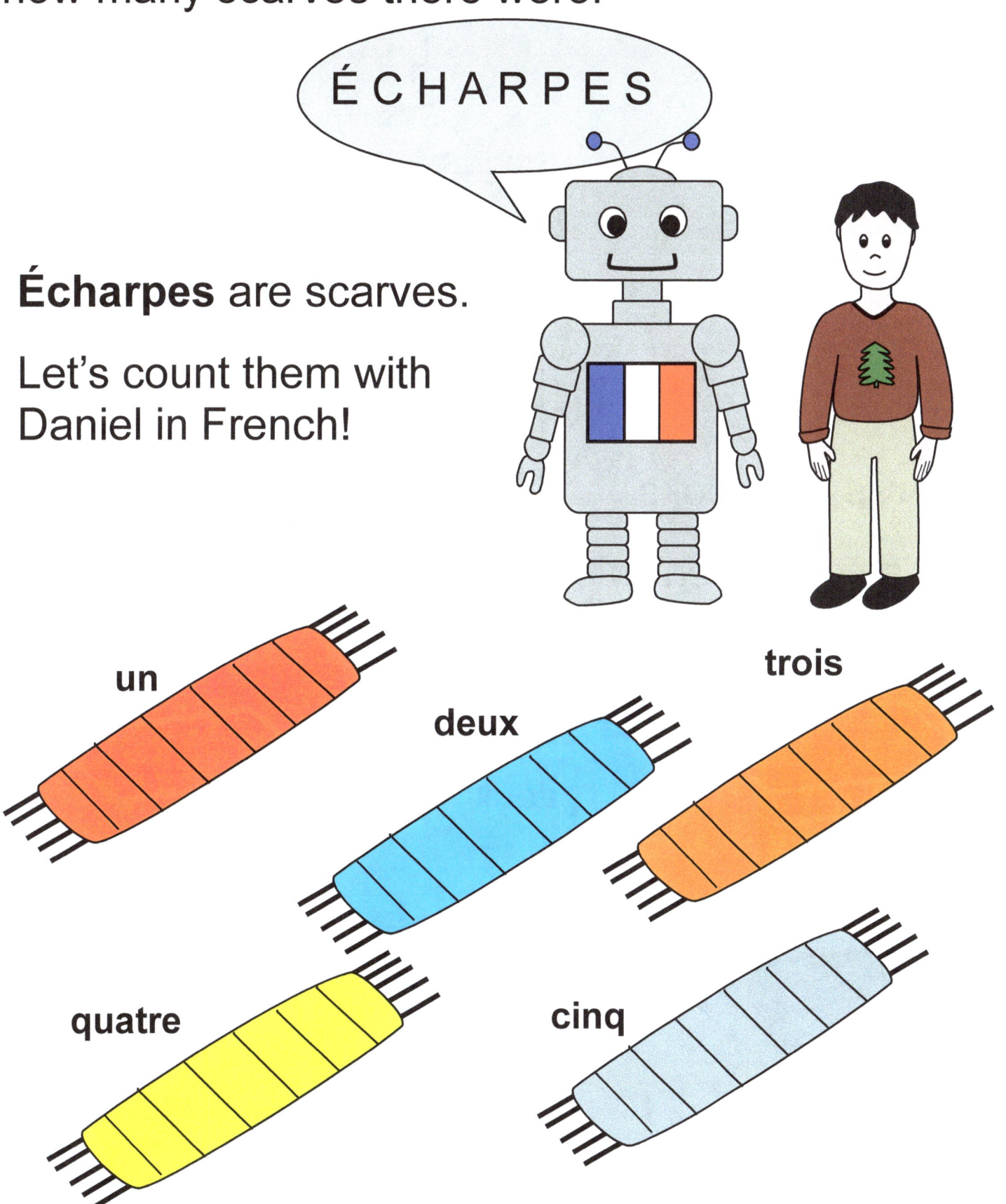

Écharpes are scarves.

Let's count them with Daniel in French!

un

deux

trois

quatre

cinq

Il y a cinq écharpes.   There are five scarves.

Next they were asked to wrap some presents. The robot knew what colour paper they needed so he told Daniel in French:

"Rouge, s'il vous plaît"

"Rouge." Thought Daniel. "What colour is **rouge**?"

Now he was helping **Père Noël** it was important he got the right coloured paper for the presents!

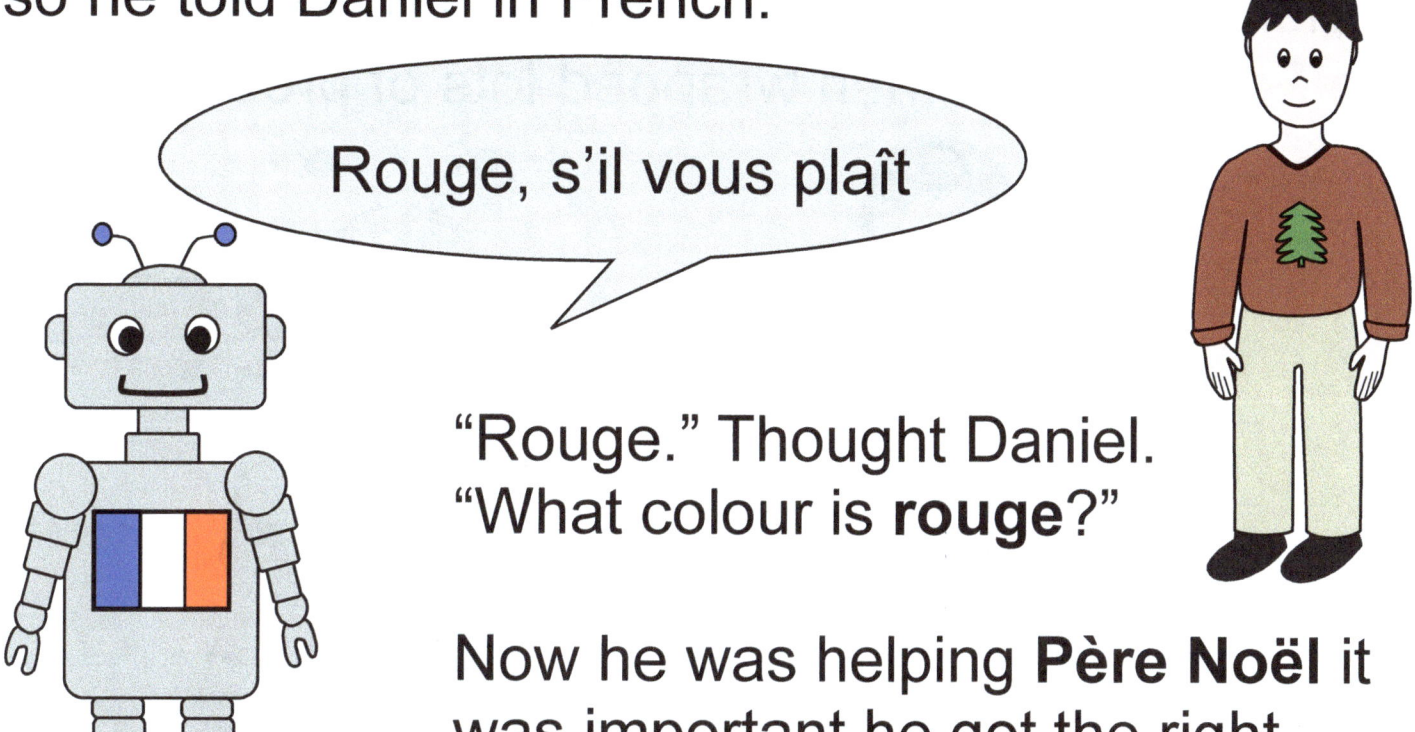

bleu **vert** **jaune** **rouge** **orange**

Daniel quickly picked up the paper which was the colour **rouge.** He was very happy he remembered that **rouge** was red. Daniel and the French robot then wrapped lots of presents:

1	2	3	4	5	6	7	8	9	10
un	deux	trois	quatre	cinq	six	sept	huit	neuf	dix

Il y a dix cadeaux. (There are ten presents.)

Père Noël was so happy that Daniel and the French robot had helped him that he asked Daniel what he'd like to take home with him today.

Now Daniel had seen lots of amazing toys but he *didn't* ask for any of these things!

Instead he said:

Un livre, s'il vous plaît.

Père Noël went away and returned with……

un livre

Père Noël brought Daniel a book all about trains.

Daniel told everyone that the book was for his dad.

C'est pour mon père.

Père Noël thought it was so lovely that Daniel had chosen something for his dad instead of himself, that he also let him choose something for his mum:

Une écharpe pour ma mère s'il vous plaît.

Père Noël went away and returned with......

Daniel was so happy that he now had all his Christmas presents. He had:

   un livre for his dad

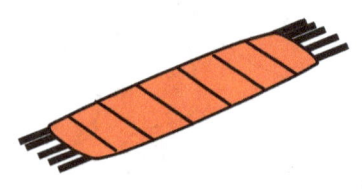   une écharpe for his mum

and

   un ballon for the French robot

The ball for the French robot was just a spare ball Daniel had, but he thought the robot would like it.

It had been a fun day and Daniel wanted to stay more but he had to be home for dinner, so they all waved goodbye and said " **Au revoir**."

French - English word list

Bonjour! --------- Hello
Au revoir! --------- Goodbye
S'il vous plaît ------- Please

Merci --------- Thank you
Regarde -------- Look
Aidez-moi ------ Help me!

Numbers

1	2	3	4	5	6	7	8	9	10
un	deux	trois	quatre	cinq	six	sept	huit	neuf	dix
one	two	three	four	five	six	seven	eight	nine	ten

Toys

un ballon — a ball
un bateau — a boat
un nounours — a teddy bear
une poupée — a doll
un vélo — a bike

Christmas presents

un livre — a book
une écharpe — a scarf

Family

mon père — my dad
ma mère — my mum

Christmas words

Père Noël — Father Christmas
le sapin — Christmas tree
cadeaux — presents

Let's sing a song!

The following words could either be sung to a made up tune, or you could try saying the words as a rap.

For inspiration of a melody to use you could hum first a nursery rhyme. How many different versions can you create using the lyrics?

 un ballon, un ballon

 un nounours, un nounours

 une poupée, une poupée

 un bateau, un bateau

 un vélo, un vélo

 un livre, un livre

une écharpe, une écharpe

 un sapin, un sapin

Follow on activity:
Take 4 pieces of paper. Write one of the below words on each piece, and do a picture.

| un nounours | un ballon | un bateau | une poupée |

Can you remember the order the toys appear in the story "Daniel's Toys"? Arrange the words in the correct order. Look at the story or the song lyrics to see if you are right!

© Joanne Leyland   First edition 2017   Second edition 2018   Third edition 2021
The word list and the song lyrics may be photocopied by the purchasing institution or individual for class or home use.
The story may not be photocopied or reproduced digitally without the prior written agreement of the author.